Tor

I0015011

Accessing The Deep Web & Dark

Web With Tor: How To Set Up Tor,

Stay Anonymous Online, Avoid

NSA Spying & Access The Deep

Web & Dark Web

Jack Jones

Table of Contents

Introduction

The technological advances that we as a society have made in the last few decades have been mind-boggling. I remember my mother telling me that when she was a child, her father told her man would never set foot on the moon. And now, there are plans in place to colonize Mars!

When we look at all the advancements made, the internet has to take top place when it comes to the development that has had the biggest impact on us as a society.

From very humble beginnings in what was essentially a messaging system, the net has grown into a giant, media rich network with the ability to connect every person on the face of the earth.

You can find out everything about a person if you know where to look. All of our data, photos, videos, etc. in the personal and business arenas are out on the web.

And the scary part is that a lot of this data is collected without your knowledge. The sites you surf, the searches you do, cookies you install, etc. all allow a very accurate picture of what your preferences are. This is why Google and Facebook show you ads related to things that you may very well be interested in – they know what you're looking for.

So, it's not just the bad guys that you have to look out for. You no doubt try to protect your personal information from those who would use it to rip you off – such as being careful when you your credit card to pay for goods online, etc.

But not everyone who is looking for information on you is trying to steal from you. Granted, they do still want your money, but this is because they want to sell you something.

Are you really happy with this kind of free-for-all when it comes to your personal information?

I, for one, am not. But for the average web user it can be tough to get around this. Every single time you make use of an application on the web or a piece of software, they expect you to agree to their terms upfront.

What most people don't know, however, is that part of these terms is to make your personal data available to the developer.

Google, for example, knows where you live, where you are hanging out, what you are looking to buy, etc. Every time you run a Google search, it is collecting more information on you.

And it is all perfectly legal. Besides which, what can you do about it anyway?

Well, one alternative is to switch up your search engine to one such as DuckDuckGo. This is a different kind of search engine because it does not collect or store your personal information at all.

For most users, however, Google will always be the go-to search engine. For starters, the risk of losing too much personal data is managed and most of those using the internet couldn't care less.

If you've been online for a while, you have no doubt had something hacked. Maybe your Facebook account, maybe your website. Maybe it was just bad luck and you ran into some top-shelf hacker who was able to break through every firewall until they gained access. After all, it wasn't your fault, was it?

I hate to break it to you, but a hacker with the skills to hack any system they want would be on to bigger and better things – they are not interested in posting porn on your Facebook page.

For the most part, most of us are small-fry that are not worth the hacker's trouble.

There are some exceptions, of course, but we'll go into that later.

If, however, you do lose your hard-earned cash to a hacker online, the chances are that you made a stupid mistake like failing to log off your Facebook when using a shared PC or choosing a password that is easy to guess.

I once hacked my mom's Facebook because it was so easy to do considering she had chosen such a simple password. The scary part is that anyone who had seen her posts on Facebook would have been able to do the same.

This section here is not about victim-shaming, please don't get me wrong. All I am trying to do is to illustrate a point – most of the time, a hack is as a result of a mistake that you have made.

But stop worrying about it – this book has been designed to make you the ultimate covert operative online. We are going to plug the information leaks and let you surf to your heart's content without giving away all your personal details.

Now, there are many ways to do this, so many, in fact, that we could write a whole series of encyclopedias on the topic. So I will concentrate on just one for this book – TOR, The Onion Routine Project.

This was initially developed for military use but is now open to all.

It puts new meaning to the phrase "incognito" when surfing the web. When used properly, TOR can help you keep your private information to yourself when surfing the web.

Are you ready to add some layers of protection?

© **Copyright 2017 by Eddington Publishing - All rights reserved.**

This document is geared towards providing exact and reliable information in regards to the topic and issue covered. The publication is sold with the idea that the publisher is not required to render accounting, officially permitted, or otherwise, qualified services. If advice is necessary, legal or professional, a practiced individual in the profession should be ordered.

- From a Declaration of Principles which was accepted and approved equally by a Committee of the American Bar Association and a Committee of Publishers and Associations.

In no way is it legal to reproduce, duplicate, or transmit any part of this document in either electronic means or in printed format. Recording of this publication is strictly prohibited and any storage of this document is not allowed unless with written permission from the publisher. All rights reserved.

The information provided herein is stated to be truthful and consistent, in that any liability, in terms of inattention or otherwise, by any usage or abuse of any policies, processes, or directions contained within is the solitary and utter responsibility of the recipient reader. Under no circumstances will any legal responsibility or blame be held against the publisher for any reparation, damages, or monetary loss due to the information herein, either directly or indirectly.

Respective authors own all copyrights not held by the publisher.

The information herein is offered for informational purposes solely, and is universal as so. The presentation of the information is without contract or any type of guarantee assurance.

The trademarks that are used are without any consent, and the publication of the trademark is without permission or backing by the trademark owner. All trademarks and brands within this book are for clarifying purposes only and are the owned by the owners themselves, not affiliated with this document.

Chapter 1

Staying Anonymous on the Deep Web

TOR is one of the solutions to keeping your personal data secure on the deep web. Let's have a look at why it's a workable solution.

This application was initially developed as a secure military communications network. Now, however, TOR servers are available to anyone online. This system protects your identity by have several routers that move traffic.

If someone runs a search on who you are, they will come up with a batch of TOR servers at random, getting them no closer to who you actually are.

The reason that the traffic is moved as it is, is so that the various nodes within the network are able to hide the person actually online – you.

This will enable you to remain anonymous in the face of the various services used to track the personal data of users.

Chapter 2

What is TOR?

So we understand basically that TOR helps you to stay anonymous and we know that it is essentially a communications network. To understand it more fully, we need to understand what it is used for as well.

What is TOR Used For?

TOR can prove to be a very handy tool. These are some of the reason why you might want to use it:

- Maybe you want to look for information that you are not meant to be looking for and need to stay anonymous.

- Maybe you need to use a shared PC and don't want to risk your data being compromised.

- Maybe you want to keep ISPs, advertisers, websites, etc. from tracking your online activity for marketing purposes.

- Maybe you want to work around the police or you are in a country that won't allow freedom of access to all information on the web.

- Perhaps you need to get your message out there without fear of recriminations.

Great, But How Does it Work?

The best analogy is an onion here. An onion is made up of a number of different layers. Each one protecting the layer beneath it. You need to work your way through these various layers in order to get to the core of the onion.

In TOR, the "layers" are the routers within the network and those wanting to find the information at the core must work their way through each of these layers.

Let's put it another way. Let's say that you need to ship a vase. You do not want it to be scratched or damaged, so you cover it with bubble wrap. You want more protection so you add a couple more layers. Then you put it into a box and place packing peanuts in there as an extra layer of protection.

The vase is very well protected. No one looking at the box would be able to see what was inside because of how it was packed. Even if someone did get to open the box and managed to take the vase out, they still couldn't see it because of the bubble wrap. Until someone persists in unwrapping each layer of bubble wrap, they are not able to see the full picture at all.

This is pretty the principle around which TOR was created. In this case, though, the vase is your data and your search history. To prevent the information being easy to track, TOR sends it through several nodes on its network. Each redirection of the traffic is like adding another layer of bubble wrap.

Nodes can consist of servers and routers worldwide and so the information can be passed on endlessly if need be.

It sounds pretty simple and it is. And the great news is that you don't have to be a techie to get the system to work for you.

Is it Secure?

It's a funny thing – this is always the first thing that I get asked. The truth is that nothing online, like in life, is ever going to be completely secure. You could run off and live in a cave to try and escape risk and get bitten on the toe by a scorpion.

TOR is also not 100% secure. Whilst it has proven to be an alternative that outperforms several others, there have been a number of weaknesses that have been found in the last few years. I have given the lists of exploits involving TOR. (These are items that hackers make use of to exploit weaknesses in a system.)

Exploits Involving TOR

- **AS Eavesdropping**: It is possible to spy on the traffic that moves into and out of the network. If the hacker is a pro, they could use this info to find out where you are.

- **Exit Node Eavesdropping**: This is the point at which the data exits the system – where the TOR hands it off to a server outside of the network. So, if you are using the TOR network to sign into a password protected server outside the network, a sophisticated hacker could get their hands on passwords or other sensitive data. It is best to use normal networks to check your emails, internet banking, etc. Avoid anything that is password protected on TOR unless it also resides on the TOR network.

- **Traffic Analysis Attack**: This is not such a huge threat but there is a chance that someone could get information about what you are doing. They should not be able to identify you though.

- **TOR Exit Node Block**: There are certain sites that will not allow users on the TOR network to fully access their sites without providing identification. Wikipedia is one such site – you can still view the information but won't be able to edit any of the pages.

- **Bad Apple Attack**: This makes use of services within the TOR that are already weak. This includes BitTorrent clients. The way a around this is simple – don't try to use TOR as a way of keeping downloads via Torrent sites anonymous.

- **Any protocol that might expose your IP address**: It's not just BitTorrent that jeopardizes your online anonymity, P2P tracker comms can also make you vulnerable. Steer clear of anything that might leave your IP address exposed.

- **Sniper Attacks**: There is very little nothing worse than an attack that leads to a denial of service. This can be done by a sophisticated hacker. They force you to use a particular set of exit nodes by blocking most nodes in the system. This allows them to figure out who you are but it is not something that amateur hackers are usually able to do.

- **Vulnerabilities with Bio Trackers**: User bio trackers can prove to be a liability within a TOR network.

- **Volume of Data**: If someone is tracking you, it is possible for them to match your activity within the TOR network by the volume of data that you are using and moving.

- **To Be Advised**: There are no doubt going to be new exploits and vulnerabilities identified as time goes on. It's not feasible to expect a system to be 100% secure all the time.

I realize that this list may make you want to think twice about the security of using the Tor network but it should be noted that there are security issues with any system. However, It should be noted that the main benefit derived from the TOR is that you can surf the web anonymously. With some additional safeguards in place, you can increase your security within the system as well.

Using TOR

Using TOR is not that hard but you do need to use a browser that will work with it. You can check the TOR Project site to get the newest releases of the tool. It is worth looking into using the TOR Project browser because it offers a simple entry to anonymous surfing.

Alternatively, you can choose to add it to your existing browser if it is compatible. Mozilla is a browser that is supported and one that you might be interested in if you are already a Mozilla user. You don't have quite as much functionality as you would have with the actual TOR browser but this is an easy option if you are not all that clued up on computers. It is as simple as adding the option to Mozilla.

The Advantages and Disadvantages of the TOR Browser

The Advantages:

- If you want the best when it comes to anonymity, it is tough to beat the browser. If you need to be able to stay private most of the time online, this is a good option. You can browse sites without leaving a trail.

- Gaining access to the Dark Web. There is a lot going on in the Dark Web. It is a zone that search engines fear to enter. It may seem enticing but it is a place where a lot of illegal deals take place. This is the place on the web where you are most likely to find things such as child pornography, murder for hire, etc. Tread lightly if you venture there because you could end up in trouble with the law.

- You'll be practically invisible to prying eyes. Your basic entry-level hacker is not going to be able to pick you up. That is not to say that you are completely safe though. A more experienced hacker might be able to find you.

- The TOR is a golden standard if you want to browse in private. It is highly mobile and allows for access to be carefully hidden.

The Disadvantages:

- If you are a stickler for performance, this is not for you. Things have been improving but it is still quite a bit slower than normal browsing. You need to decide if the increase in privacy is worth sacrificing a bit of speed.

- You won't be completely secure and you could be monitored. It should be kept in mind that state agencies monitor online activity that attempts to remain hidden. If you stumble onto a site related to illegal activities even just once, they will be monitoring you. If you are a repeat customer, they may become very interested in you. That said, don't panic too much if you find an illegal site in error. As long as you act in the correct way, you will be okay. That means that you need to get off the site as quickly as possible or make a report about the site to the relevant authorities. If you do get asked questions, be open and honest with your answers.

- There have been issues with people misusing the network because of the anonymity it provides. Reputationally, the TOR network has taken a beating. That said, not all of the activity deemed illegal is wrong. For example, many activists living in societies where there is a lot of censorship have made use of the TOR network to get their message across.

- Latency issues abound on the TOR network. You are going to need to suck it up and be patient here or avoid using this network altogether.

The Advantages and Disadvantages of the Mozilla Add-On

If you decide to go for the Mozilla add-on instead, here is what you can expect.

- Mozilla products are all free and open-source and anyone can help to improve them. The developers have ensured that people are easily able to check that the system does deliver what it claims to. Transparency helps keep the developers honest.

- You can customize the add-on as you like. That means that you can have a browsing experience that is set to your own specifications.

- You do get access to a very supportive community. For a beginner, this is most important. You can get access to assistance from various members of the community.

- Mozilla works across a range of platforms and will work with many different operating systems. If you upgrade your device in future, you are able to enjoy continuity of service because of this – you don't have to go and learn a whole new software version again.

- In addition, the add-on is constantly being improved upon. It supports HTML5, allows you to sync your data across different devices, let's you set up and manage bookmarks and has a function that allows for the quick grab of pages. It features a lower drain on your computer's resources in terms of CPU usage and memory.

- One annoyance is that you need to restart the system with every new extension that you install.

- The speed of operations is not consistent over all operating systems. It is slower when using a Mac than it would be in Linux or Windows.

- The speed at which Mozilla is being developed could end up leaving the extension behind. Extensions may not continue to work with newer versions of the browser.

Chapter 3

Will TOR work for you?

It is not always appropriate to use the TOR network. You need to draw the line between maintaining safety and anonymity online. The TOR network is not perfect and is very much still a work in progress.

And whilst the protocol underlying the TOR remains unbroken, the fact that you have to use it within a browser introduces a level of vulnerability. And browsers are not great a strong link in the chain of internet security.

Your browser is what allows you to connect with the network online but it can be exploited. It has been said that certain government agencies are able to identify and track users of the TOR network.

What that essentially means is that using the TOR system is not going to completely protect you if you want to hide illegal activity. It   might make things harder on the authorities trying to find you but it won't stop them forever.

That means that illegal usage of this system is not recommended. In fact, if you have nefarious intentions, you should steer well clear of the system – if someone else in the community finds you, they are bound to report you to maintain the integrity of the online community using the network.

Avoid doing the following when on the TOR network:

- Trying to download big files if you want to retain anonymity. You will need to use some kind of torrent client and this will make it easy to track what you have downloaded. It will take longer than normal and slow the network down for everyone. And there really is nothing to gain from it.

- Trying to avoid being surveilled by a government agency. The federal government agencies are able to access the network and identify users. You are not really anonymous to them, even on the TOR network.

- Trying to stay safe online while accessing your social media accounts. The very act of accessing your social media means that you have to move off the TOR network and lose anonymity anyway. Furthermore, your access details will be exposed when you leave the network. It is not safe to surf sites that you need password access to on the TOR network.

- Accessing official websites or system. Every such access is logged and can be traced. Most people trying to access such sites are doing so for nefarious reasons. In addition to which, it is an offence to attempt unauthorized access to any site and you are risking some serious jail time if you are caught. It might be tempting, considering how anonymous you feel but this is not what TOR was originally designed for.

- There are lots of reasons to use the TOR network but you do need to bear in mind that the very fact that you are using an anonymous service like this will raise red flags for law enforcement agencies.

Chapter 4

Your Step By Step Guide to Getting Started with TOR

Right, are you ready to start?

Is TOR for You?

We've been through the fact that TOR will not be a good fit for everyone. The first step anyone should take is to ensure that TOR is really going to work for you.

We are not going to go through a list of pros and cons, though. We are going to look at best practices that you may need to implement if you want to use TOR.

Changing the Operating System

Windows is meant to be easy to use, even for the most unskilled user. A problem with this approach is that it is also a lot easier to hack. There are many exploits out there designed specifically around Windows.

And remember, TOR only protects your identity, it does not make your system more secure. It could pay you to change over to an operating system that is more secure, such as Linux. Linux works well with TOR.

You will also find that Mac has better security than windows and also works with TOR. Just keep in mind that the TOR network is usually slower for Mac users.

Stay Up to Date

Yes, I know those endless updates are extremely annoying but you must ensure that your operating system, browser and anti-virus programs are regularly updated. Every update has been put in place for a reason – and it could be a security reason.

HTTPS Everywhere

How many sites have you been on that don't offer HTTPS? These sites are not properly encrypted and could be dangerous to visit. An add-on for your browser known as "HTTPS Everywhere" can solve that problem for you by switching to the encrypted version of the site, where it is supported.

Data Encryption

It seems rather silly to go to all the trouble of surfing anonymously if you do not benefit in terms of increased security as well. If you are running a Linux system, you can look for TrueCrypt and LUKS to encrypt your data for you.

TOR Bundle is Not the Best Idea

It might seem as though TOR Bundle puts together the best in anonymity and security but this is a misperception that could cost you dearly.

The bundle does offer an additional layer but the FBI has pointed out that there are vulnerabilities here as well. It is best not to rely on TOR Bundle for all your security.

No More Java, Java Script and Flash

The problem with these scripts is that they could be sharing your information without any consideration about whether it is what you want to do or not. Turn these off so that your private browsing history is not shared.

No More Peer-to-Peer

Yes, I have said this a few times now. But I really want to stress the importance of this – when using this type of connection, you are potentially putting your information at risk.

Be a Cookie Monster

Cookies are in place to monitor your behavior on a particular site and store personal data. If you want to be truly anonymous, install an add-on such as Self-Destructing Cookies. These add-ons will delete the cookies.

Use Fake Accounts

You go to all the trouble of installing TOR, changing your operating system and deleting cookies as you go, and then you use your real email address. Congratulations, you have now just announced to everyone who you are. Set up a fake email account to use while in the TOR network.

Bye Bye Google

You know when they say, "Big brother is watching", they might as well be referring to Google. Google is one of the worst offenders when it comes to collecting data about you personally. Rather use a search engine that does not collect data such as StartPage or DuckDuckGo.

Act Legally

Be sure to stick to the rules when surfing anonymously. State and federal law enforcement agencies monitor anonymous users and are quick to act when illicit activities are flagged. Steer clear of sites that are less than legal.

There are some instances, however, when it is wiser to use TOR when conducting "illegal" activities. If, for example, you are living in a country where the media is heavily censored and you want to keep an eye on international media without being monitored.

Choose Whether to Use the TOR Browser or an Add-On

So now you have made your decision – you have decided that TOR will work well for you.

We have been through the advantages and disadvantages of either course of action and so you have no doubt made a decision as to which is the preferred option for you. Who knows, maybe you've decided that you'll make use of both.

Stepping Behind the Curtain

You are almost ready to step inside TOR. First of all, make sure that you have physically logged out of any applications that you have on your system. If you do not do this, you run the risk of them sharing your data whilst in TOR.

Once you have done that, where do you start to explore? Here are some suggestions.

Hidden Wiki

This is the TOR version of Wikipedia. You can use it to find items that you are interested in. This site lists what hidden onion sites there are and lists what topics are covered. To find Hidden Wiki is simple – just access your DuckDuckGo search engine to search for it. You'll find it quite easily that way.

What you could find:

- **News**: Getting uncensored news is one of the primary, more legitimate uses of TOR. You are able to find all the most up to date news. There are several sites within the TOR network devoted to giving up to date news. All you need to do is to find one that is credible and that is of interest to you.

- **Introduction Points**: These can be considered stepping stones. They bridge the gap between the "normal" web and the TOR sites. These will be the first sites that you come across within the network.

- **Commercial Services**: There are going to be times when you want to buy something completely anonymously. Bitcoins can be used here and this makes it possible for transactions to be conducted entirely anonymously. The transactions can be traced but it will take someone with excellent skills to do so when you are within the TOR network.

- **History**: Despite what you may have been taught in school, history can be more a matter of perspective than of actual fact. As they say, history is in the hands of the winners. If, for example, the Nazis had won World War II, what would we have been taught of the Holocaust today? Searching through TOR, you are more likely to find actual personal accounts, etc. that have not been spun to look good.

- **Forums**: Are you desperate to discuss how bad your government is but scared of recriminations? You could join an online community within the TOR system. Google, etc. has similar forums but it is not nearly as easy to remain anonymous with these. The developers of these forums on the normal web have full access to your IP address, real user name and email address (even if these are hidden from the rest of the community) and they can be compelled to hand that information over.

- **Dangerous Topics**: The anonymity of the TOR system is obviously a huge drawcard for those who are conducting illicit activities. There are many sites that will teach you how to create viruses, how to hack systems, create malware, etc. It is better to steer clear of these sites to avoid getting into trouble with the authorities. This may be difficult to do as some of these sites will pop-up on your screen. If you do come across them by accident or by pop-up, don't get drawn in - you just need to close them as quickly as possible.

For most uses, however, the Hidden Wiki is going to give you all the information that you need. The lists on the site may not always be current but it is still the best source of information about what is on the TOR network.

Sites within the TOR network are not always maintained or as long-lasting as those outside of the network.

It is a good idea to set up bookmarks when you find a site that you want to visit again. Unlike the normal web, URLS on the TOR network are difficult to remember. In addition, you cannot always rely on the directories within the Hidden Wiki either. This might mean having to do some serious searching to find a site again. Bookmark it to be on the safe side.

Onion Chat

Onion Chat refers to anonymous chat rooms on the TOR network. Because of the anonymity aspect, they are more likely to remain in service for longer. You can even make friends during these chats.

That said, however, it should always be a priority to guard your identity – use a nickname and never reveal information about yourself that could let them figure out who you are. It would be unwise to tell someone which town you live in, where you work, etc.

New Yorker Strongbox

News agencies often rely on insider information when it comes to blowing scandals wide open. The New Yorker maintains a site on the TOR network to allow people who want to give them tips to do so completely anonymously. They assign you a code name and never force you to reveal who you actually are. (Though, if you are hoping to get paid, you will have to reveal this at some stage.)

It Can be Lonely In the TOR

TOR is not a network that everyone knows about and it is not someone that everyone knows how to use. There is a sense of being alone on the network because those who have sites and blogs may not make regular posts.

Users of TOR are looking for anonymity and so may not want to interact with you. In addition, websites within the network tend to be of a more transient nature.

Unlike the normal web, there is not going to be someone trying to sell you something every five minutes and finding information is not necessarily going to be quick and easy.

Knowing that upfront means that you understand that you have to exercise patience and be more resourceful than usual. The latency problems with the system can also cause a lot of irritation.

It is the tradeoff that you make for being able to surf anonymously.

Best Practices

Here we will go through what you can do to get the most out of using TOR on a regular basis, especially when it comes to navigating the system and communicating within it.

Browsing Safely

TOR will not connect with Google by design. What it does is to connect to a page that basically interacts with Google on your behalf. This prevents Google from being able to make logs of whatever you have searched for. (Ever wonder how you always seem to see ads that are so on point after Googling something?

Google makes notes of what you search for and ensures that it displays ads related to your search preferences.)

Because the TOR network puts this page in between you and Google, Google is not able to attribute the search to any particular person. It makes it impossible to trace by simple means accessible to most users. (Not counting governmental agencies, of course.)

Where TOR cannot do anything is when it comes to the sites, scripts and any extensions that are run. If you are using the TOR browser, it will disable information-gathering scripts, etc. by default. It is not a good idea to mess with this default setting at all or you risk exposing your identity.

It should also be realized that, due to the privacy settings, some applications may not run as well as they should. For example, Flash protocols are disabled on the TOR network and so you might not be able to watch your favorite YouTube channel, for example.

Some streaming of YouTube has been made possible with the HTML5 additions YouTube has made but this is still in the early stages.

Where TOR does excel, however, is in warning you which files or documents might compromise your identity. And it tends to be pretty accurate so it is best to take such warnings to heart.

Anonymous Messaging

When it comes to the normal web, anonymous messaging is impossible. Even if you are using nicknames, all your personal information, including your IP address, etc. is on record with the company offering the service.

In addition, all messaging services log your chats and monitor them. Which essentially means that nothing is really private anymore.

That's where making use of the TOR system can also be very effective. TorChat is a messaging app that can be used as a simple extension. All you need to do is to download the app from the site and run the executable file to install it.

The app works exactly as your normal messaging programs do and is very user-friendly. The primary difference is that you are assigned a name by the system that consists of a random number of characters.

You are able to assign nicknames to people on your list so that you know who you are speaking to.

And, because the system runs on the TOR network, it is not possible to easily trace your real identity, nor will anyone else be able to establish who you are speaking to.

Crypto Messaging

Should you want to go all 007 here, you can also encrypt your messages and then send them through the TOR network.

The problem here is that there is a greater chance that the messages can be intercepted because the apps that allow encryption won't work in the background. However, because the messages are encrypted, anyone who intercepts them will find them difficult to read. A service like Cryptocat is a good option here and it can be downloaded from the Cryptocat site.

Emails That are Truly Anonymous

What happens when instant messages are no good? What if you must send an email? The TOR network does have a hidden email service but you have to be within the network to make use of it.

In order to access it, you just need to go to the site while on the TOR network and set it up from there.

The service is very user-friendly and intuitive to use. It looks similar to your usual online mail clients. The big advantage is that it is impossible to access it or search through the messages unless you are in the TOR network.

Step-by-Step Guide to TOR

Go to the official site and find the Browser download page. In Windows, this is quite easy – you usually just need to hit the download button and allow it to be installed. If you are running a different operating system, you should follow the developer's instructions for that system.

Here is a more technical breakdown of the process for you:

This is for those who are more technically minded and who want to run through the process one step at a time.

TOR Browser Installation with the Windows Operating System

As mentioned above, it is pretty simple to install the browser into windows.

1. Close all programs other than your web browser.

2. Start at the official TOR website and look for the updated version of the browser. On the top right-hand side of the screen you will see a tab for Downloads. Click on this.

3. Now select the operating system you are using. The options you can choose from include Apple, Window, Source Code, Smartphones and Linux so you can download it to your laptop, tablet or smartphone – or all of your devices if you like.

4. Select your language preference in order to begin the download. You will be given the option of also downloading TOR Bundle – a toolset aimed at making it easier to improve your privacy when you are surfing. (Just remember what I mentioned earlier about not relying solely on the TOR Bundle for this. Do take the other steps to further increase your safety while browsing.)

5. You will be asked where you want to save the actual installed files on your device. This is not a major issue as it has little effect on how the rest of the process goes. (Just ensure that you have enough memory on the device so that you can install the files.)

6. As soon as the download is complete, you can open it so that it can install the browser. If you decide to do this later on, you will need to find the files in the location that you had chosen earlier.

7. Select the appropriate language that you want to use and then press the OK button.

8. You will again need to choose where the files will run from. Again, make sure the memory is adequate for this. (A pop-up window will come up with a suggested download path, showing how much memory is needed and how much is available. If you want it installed to a different location, hit the "Browse" button and choose the location that you want, otherwise continue as normal.)

9. Leave the installer to do its thing – this will take a few minutes.

10. You will be asked if you want to also install a link in the start menu and if you want to create a shortcut on the desktop. The decision is

yours. Once that decision is made, the browser is fully installed and ready to use.

Using TOR Through BlackBelt Privacy on Firefox

1. If you would rather use the software through Firefox, you can use BlackBelt to help you do this. You will need to have the Firefox browser as well so if you don't have it, download it now.

2. Search for BlackBelt Privacy + TOR and download the latest version. It won't take long because it's a very small file.

3. Open the file and then choose one of the following options:

TOR Client Only Operator – this enables you to use the TOR network but doesn't allow others to use you as a relay.

Bridge Relay Operator – This enables you to use the TOR network and to also act as a relay so that others can do the same.

Censored User – If you are using this to avoid censorship at home, this should be the option that you choose.

4. Once you have selected what kind of TOR user you want to be, you can carry on with installing the program.

5. As soon as it is installed, you can start browsing anonymously.

Setting it Up Manually

1. If something goes wrong and the configuration does not seem to be working as it should, you can try the following manual settings.

2. You need to have installed the TOR browser before starting, so do that now.

3. Despite the fact that we have installed the browser, we are not going to use it to navigate, we are going to use Mozilla instead. (Mozilla is updated more frequently than the TOR browser and this means improved and more up to date security.)

4. Once TOR is installed, open up your Mozilla browser and click on the settings button – you want to choose Proxy settings.

5. If you want to do the same for Windows, go to your Menu, select Options, choose Advanced Options, find Network and then go to Settings.

6. From there are the process is that same for both – you are going to manually set the proxies. Do this as follows: SOCKS Host: 127.0.0.1; Port Box: 9150 and, if given the option, choose SOCKS v5. Check that the Remote DNS box has been checked. After No Proxy for introduce: 127.0.0.1.

7. Now check if the TOR is working. If so, you will receive a message to say that you are navigating anonymously. If not, you will receive a message that your IP address is detectable.

8. If it is still not working, it is better to deactivate it completely and see if you can walk through the troubleshooting process.

How to Set Up Hidden Services

Are you intrigued by using hidden services within the TOR network? Does it sound like fun? What if you set your own up?

What is nice is that it is relatively simple to set up your very own hidden service within the TOR network.

For this to work, you must first install the TOR browser on your device.

After that, you need to set up a local server to use. According the TOR experts, Windows users should try using Savant and Max or Linux users should try using thttpd Web Server.

You can choose a different server if you like but do keep in mind that this may open you up to a different set of vulnerabilities.

Open up the configuration and select HTTP first, from there select Server DNS. Type in the word "localhost" and, where it says "Port # To Serve From" type in "80".

Your usual path for Savant in Windows is: C:
\Savant\Root directory. You need to ensure that the
default used by Savant is replaced by your
"Index.html" document.

You can see whether or not things are running as they
should by opening your browser and typing
"localhost" into it.

To check that everything is running correctly, you just
need to type localhost in the browser. You can use a
different port if you want – set it up by entering
"localhost:[#of the port]". So, you could for example,
type "localhost:125 for port # 125".

You have now brought the local server up online and can set up your hidden service.

All that you need to do is to let the TOR browser know that you have set up a new server. This can be done by: Closing your TOR browser as needed; Typing "torrc" into your computer's search function (You can also look to see if it is in the Tor directory on your computer); Opening this file using a simple editor like Notepad; Adding in some text such as: # Hidden Service; HiddenServiceDir C: \Users\Name\tor_service; HiddenServicePort 80 127.0.0.1:80.

You then need to go into C:\Users\Name\tor_service string and change this to an actual path set on your computer.

You should not use a website to use as a directory here. You will have to match the final number in the new string to the port you chose earlier when setting up the local server.

If you do not have a tor_service folder, create a new folder for it. Save your changes and then restart the browser again.

You would then need to check through your message log to ensure that everything went smoothly with the configuration.

There are going to be 2 documents in the tor_service folder – private_key and hostname.

These make sure that your service functions as it should and so should be kept safe. If someone gets their hand on the key, they can use it to delete the hidden service you have set up.

If you open the hostname file, you will see the hidden address's onion address. This is what you can share with those that you want to be able to use the service.

You have now set up a TOR site and can post what you like to it. Visitors to the site will have to be on the TOR network in order to use it.

So, it really isn't too difficult to set up a service within the TOR network. You can thus post news, etc. and share as you like with other TOR users. This is a very easy way to create a website on TOR. If you want something that looks great though, you may need to learn more about CSS and HTML.

But that is something outside the scope of this book. Tutorials on creating websites abound online and so you should have no problems finding one. There are also tons of free, generic templates that can be customized to your own needs if that is what you are looking for.

Tips to Make TOR Run Better

- No Torrents or Peer-to-peer sharing. These will work a lot more slowly in TOR and so you will hold up everyone. In addition, your IP address is revealed when doing so and that kind of makes the whole anonymity aspect void.

- Disable plug-ins for the browser unless you have personally developed them. Even when working within the TOR network, if info-gathering plug-ins have been installed, they will continue to collect data about what you have been doing.

- Always use HTTPS and don't visit sites that don't support this functionality. It is the entry and exit points to the TOR system that are most likely to be problematic when it comes to keeping your identity secret. Whilst on the network, your identity is protected, but that is not the case when moving off or onto the network. You can counter this through the proper use of encryption. If you use the add-on HTTPS Everywhere, you are going to be able to further protect your information. Sites that do not support secure HTTP protocols should be avoided completely.

- Wait until after exiting the TOR network to read documents that you may have downloaded. The potential problem is that many of these documents are stored in the cloud and may need user verification to open. A click will take you to the correct page and your system may automatically log you in to Adobe Reader, for example, giving away your identity.

It is best not to click on links that will open anything while on the network.

- Make use of bridges. The TOR system allows you to make use of a number or relays instead of interacting directly with sites. Be sure that you make use of these to further protect your identity while surfing.

- Get your friends to come on board. The more people that use the TOR network, the stronger it becomes. Tell people about it and the advantages of using it and get them to try it out for themselves.

Chapter 5

Where to Go and What to See on the Deep Web

I just want to preface this by saying that exploring the deep web can seem exciting but it's important to remember that some of what you will come across is highly illegal. There are some pretty sick people out there and you might come across things that you really don't want to see.

In addition, you could end up getting yourself into a lot of trouble with the law if you get involved in any of the illicit activities in the deep web. At times, such as when it comes to unintentionally viewing illicit material such as child pornography, the act of just seeing the site can get you into trouble regardless of your intentions. So, even if you are not actually intending to get involved with anything illegal on the deep web, you stand the chance of getting into trouble.

The best way to protect yourself in situations such as these is to immediately get off the site. You should also consider reporting the matter to the relevant authorities.

For your own sake, do not use the TOR network to solicit crimes or commit crimes. As I have mentioned several times before, the authorities are on the lookout for this kind of thing.

Using Hidden Services

Hidden services are regularly used within the TOR network because they add another level of privacy. Websites using such services are not subject to being spied upon in the same way as normal sites are.

This makes them less likely to be able to be blocked or spammed. They can theoretically run indefinitely because there is no way for outsiders to take them down.

Let's look at a real-world example here. Say, for example, I am annoyed with a company and I want to cause them real harm. If I could get enough people on my side, we could spam the company's site until it crashed.

It would take some effort but it would be possible to do because, on the normal internet, their servers, etc. would be fairly easy to find. It would then be a matter of throwing enough data at them to overload their capacity.

If, on the other hand, they could keep their services hidden, I would not be able to spam the site and crash it.

With the TOR network, the servers are anonymous and so less vulnerable to attack. As a result, you will be able to use the services every day. Anonymity can also be valuable to those wanting to transfer things like Bitcoins in secret.

Making Use of Bookmarks

Where all the anonymity can become annoying is when you want to find a site that you have visited before. Sites on the TOR network don't have a typical URL. You are not going to find something like Amazon.com. Instead, you will find something more along the lines of armjagsgdgada.onion.

That makes it pretty hard to remember the address of sites that you have visited. In addition, the pages within the deep web are not indexed as normal web pages are so keyword searches are not as helpful.

Finding a site then might actually depend more on luck. If you do find a site that you'll want to visit again, bookmark it. You can always delete the bookmark later if you want to.

Finding Information in the Deep Web

We've already spoken a bit about Hidden Wiki as a means of finding sites of interest in the deep web. The Hidden Wiki does, however, share only information that is considered safe for general consumption.

TorSearch is another way to find information.

It works similarly to Google except that it doesn't track your personal searches. It has also made it a lot easier to find things in the deep web.

Issues that You May Encounter

Anonymity is one thing. Online security is something else. When using the TOR network you run the risk of being exposed to vulnerabilities. Experienced hackers may still be able to track you.

In addition, you might also be exposing yourself to viruses – after all, not everyone using the deep web is there with good intentions, are they?

You also need to assume that you are being monitored when using the TOR network. Whilst it may be harder for normal people to track you, governmental agencies are able to do so. And are more likely to do so because you are using the network. This means that you have to be really careful about what sites you click on.

Being Careful in the Deep Web

There are some search engines that are available in the deep web but you do need to be circumspect about which you choose.

For example, there is a search engine called Grams that has garnered a lot of interest from authorities because of its relation to drugs and online dealing of the same.

There are several online markets within the TOR network as well. These include Agora, Middle Earth and Evolution to name but a few.

Middle Earth tends to be more user-friendly. Evolution and Agora, on the other hand, tend to be more reliable and this makes them a more popular choice.

It is very important, before you make any kind of purchase within the TOR network that you understand exactly how it is going to work. You also need to understand the possible implications of buying what it is that you are buying, especially if it is of an illegal nature.

When it comes to paying for goods, one thing you never want to do here is to give anyone your personal information. You can get around this by using Bitcoins. For this you will need a Bitcoin wallet and to purchase Bitcoins. This can be done on the official Bitcoin site.

Bitcoins are a cryptocurrency and are the safest way to exchange money in the TOR network.

It can be just as tough making a decision about whether or not a site is trustworthy as it is on the normal internet. Look for references from other clients before completing the purchase and, when in doubt, don't go through with it.

Concerns About Content

Because of the nature of the content in the TOR network, a general web search can be more of a risk than a normal web search would be.

Here are some of the things that you have to look out for in the TOR network:

Unlinked Content: There is no indexing of sites by a search engine. You will not be able to find links or backlinks on the sites.

Dynamic Content: These sites will require you to have some knowledge of how domains work in order for you to access them. They might require you to send queries while navigating.

Private Webs: These are essentially membership sites. You need to be circumspect about such sites because you will be required to give personal information in order to become a member. There are fake sites out there designed to get hold of your personal information.

Contextual Webs: These sites may require different access contexts. For example, they might place reliance on prior clients here.

Limited Access Content: Systematically these sites tend to be more difficult for search engines to index.

They have CAPTCHAs, etc. in place to ensure that they are less vulnerable to robots.

Scripted Content: These websites require the use of JavaScript or Flash software, for example. As mentioned previously, such scripts can be used to gather personal information.

Software Driven Content: You need to have the correct program or app installed to gain access here.

Web Archives: These will often let you look at previous incarnations of websites. This can be used to see what previous versions of sites were in place.

The TOR network contains many different formats online just as your normal browsing does. The key to keeping safe here is that you understand what the different formats are and how they might affect you.

Just like the regular internet, you don't want to download files that can create changes on your computer or files that you just randomly come across.

What is the Future of the Deep Web?

In the last few years, the numbers of people using the TOR network has been steadily increasing. There has also been an uptake of people trying to escape political censorship, as can be seen during the events of the Arab spring.

Activism is one large reason for resorting to the use of TOR but there has also been an uptake of people who just want to be able to experience the internet free of censorship.

The truth is though that there are unplumbed depths when it comes to the deep web. How much information there actually is, is anyone's guess.

Getting an accurate estimate to the actual amount of information is difficult because of the nature of the network itself. What is known is that the number of users has increased substantially.

It no longer takes a range of skills to be able to make use of the deep web – you can set up your own hidden services in a matter of minutes. And, if you're not sure of how to get more out of the web, you can easily consult an online tutorial.

More and more people are looking to be able to surf anonymously – whether that is in an effort to conceal illicit activities or in a misguided attempt to feel more secure online.

It should never be forgotten that as the system becomes more and more popular, it will become more of a target for hackers looking to score personal information.

There are not the normal safeguards in place – you are anonymous but that doesn't mean you are completely safe. In fact, it may be more dangerous for the uninitiated because it is so unregulated – even if you come across a scamming website, shutting it down is easier said than done.

Considering how easy it is for scammers online already, the deep web can be like the old wild west – if you're not careful, you'll end up being a victim.

You could end up being scammed because there are lots of sites out there itching to take your money. And there is little to no recourse if you do get scammed.

But, in the grand scheme of things, is it really so different in the regular online world? As long as you are aware of the potential risk, you are far better able to keep yourself safe.

It might be safer to stay out of the deep web but it's safer in the same way as it would be to never leave your home. Sure, if you don't set foot out the door, you are not likely to get hit by a bus but you're not going to have any fun either.

But, if you set out each day, aware of how to keep yourself safe, you can have new and exciting experiences.

Who's to say that the TOR network is not the next evolution in the development of the internet? Who's to say that in a few years' time we won't all crave the anonymity that came before Facebook and Twitter became such a big part of our lives?

If you told someone fifty years ago that you could have a face to face conversation with someone on the other side of the planet, they would have thought you were mad but today we have Skype and video calls.

Our grandparents would never have imagined a world where just about everything could be ordered by clicking on a few sites online. Who knows what our future will be like and who knows what role a TOR network might play in that?

Concerns About Privacy

Privacy is something that is hard to come by in the modern world. News breaks instantly across the world and is discussed many times over. In minutes news on social media and from there it spreads virally. This can be a good thing.

But, on a personal level, our own privacy has never become more precious. Social media makes it all but impossible to keep secrets anymore.

I'll cite an incident from my own life as an example. My brother and his ex-wife have a very acrimonious relationship. The same can be said of her and the rest of our family. She has blocked all members of the family from her Facebook page.

Anyway, the one weekend my nephew was visiting, I posted a picture of him on my Facebook page – only to have her comment on it. I didn't even realize she would see it and I didn't want her commenting. Now, I have since changed my privacy settings but it made it very clear that privacy has taken on a new meaning now.

Despite the fact that I was not connected to her on Facebook on a one-to-one level, she was connected through a third person and so had access to my news.

So, yes, I can understand the increased desire for privacy. I can understand why people would want to work within the TOR network.

The TOR network is a tool like any other. It can be used for good or evil, just like any other. As and of itself, it is neither good nor evil, it really depends on how you use it.

Do services like this have a future on the internet where just about everything is monitored? Yes, because people do have some desire for privacy.

Will it be misused? Of course, there are always people who will look for an easy answer.

Can it be a tool for great good? The answer, again, is yes. Think to a few years ago when Egypt cut off all access to the internet for its people. Think about countries where it is illegal to access general information because of extreme censorship.

And think of the possibilities for a low cost communication system that can truly be deemed private. Think about surfing the web without worrying about how all your personal data is being used for marketing purposes.

The internet has proven to be a source of great information and the deep web can help with this. All that is needed is to introduce some sort of regulation to it so that those misusing the system can be brought to book.

Used responsibly, the deep web is a very powerful tool.

Conclusion

The idea of exploring unknown territory is exciting but there is so much more that you gain from the TOR network. Designed to facilitate unfettered communication, this allows you to truly experience online freedom.

How you use that freedom is up to you but I hope that you look on this as a great opportunity.

Learning about the TOR network and having my own forays into the deep web was an eye-opening experience for me. And it was all a lot easier than I could ever have imagined.

I hope that this book has given you the confidence to explore on your own and that you are now willing to look around the deep web for yourself.

Have fun!

A message from the author,

Jack Jones

FREE BONUS!

As a free bonus, I've included a preview of some of my other best-selling books directly after this section. Enjoy!

FREE BONUS!: Preview Of **"Hacking** - The Complete Beginner's Guide To Computer Hacking: How To Hack Networks and Computer Systems, Information Gathering, Password Cracking, System Entry & Wireless Hacking"!

If you enjoyed this book, I have a little bonus for you; a preview of one of my other books. If you enjoy what you read, the full book is available on Amazon as an ebook or printed book.

Introduction

Have you always wondered about how hacking works? In the movies it seems so simple. All you need is some basic information and some kickass software and you can hack any network you like.

In reality, it's not quite as simple as that. Successful hacking is a combination of using the right tools, a well-planned strategy and applying some basic common sense.

In this book, we will go step by step through strategies that work and over the tools you will need to become a successful hacker.

We'll wade through the lingo used by hackers and teach you how you can get your hands on the information that you need to hack different systems.

We go through applications and software that make the task a lot easier for you and how you can determine what passwords are being used.

We end off with a short lesson on wireless hacking.

By the time we are done, you will have the skills you need to hack the networks that you want to.

And, what if you don't want to use these newly acquired skills to acquire information illegally?

Ethical hackers are a subset of hackers that utilize their skills to pinpoint weaknesses in security systems. They can show companies whether or not their systems are vulnerable.

Perhaps this is something that you can start to do – for yourself or your own company. Learning to think like a hacker does will help you to ensure that your own computer network is as secure as possible.

Chapter 1

How Hacking Works

There is something of a mystique about hackers that the world finds interesting. Hackers are portrayed by Hollywood as the cool kid version of geeks. They are portrayed as rebels who break into systems just to prove that they can. As non-conformists.

No information is safe from this Hollywood portrayal of cool kids. All they have to do is to run a piece of software or to punch out some commands on the keyboard to gain access to even the most secure information.

The truth is that it is not quite that simple. Hackers in the real world have to find ways to exploit weaknesses in the security systems of the networks that they are trying to hack.

They have to be able think both laterally and logically to get around top-flight security systems.

The good news is that it is not that hard to learn to become a hacker. You don't have to be the Hollywood rebel or the geeky teenage genius to be able to do so.

You can learn to think like a hacker and learn what tools they use. You can use this information to either get up to mischief on your own or to help secure your own private network. The choice is yours.

Understanding Hackers

The first step is to start understanding what kinds of hackers there are. People get into hacking for a range of different reasons. The first step towards understanding hackers is to understand what kind of hacker they are.

Hackers – A Basic Classification

- **White Hat Hackers**: People who have no intention of actually causing harm or stealing information fall under this category. For the most part, hackers that fall under this category will work in the security industry, testing systems for vulnerability. They look at how easy a system is to hack and work out ways to increase the protection for the system. They will usually ask for permission from the owner of the systems that they plan to hack before they start to attack it. If you have good intentions when it comes to hacking, it is important that you get permission from the system owners before going ahead. Not doing so can land you in hot water.

- **Black Hat Hackers**: Hackers that fall into this category are generally out to cause harm or steal information. They may aim to cause damage to the system by deleting important information as a purely malicious act. They might also look to steal information that they can profit from – such as credit card numbers. One particularly nasty black hat trick is to take over control of a system and prevent the rightful users from accessing it. They then make the system owners pay them to restore control. When people say that you need to protect yourself against hackers, these are the hackers that they are referring to.

- **Gray Hat Hackers**: Like everything else in life, there are various shades between black and white. This kind of hacker usually gets into it out of curiosity or just to prove that they can. They hack without malicious intent and without any desire to act in any manner that is illegal. (Apart from the hack itself, of course.) These hackers often also turn their skills towards helping system owners protect themselves against black hat hackers. The lines fudge a little because they might hack systems without anyone's express consent for reasons of their own.

What Skills You Need as a Hacker

Skilling yourself as a hacker means that you need to understand how computer systems operate. This means an extensive knowledge of programming, operating systems and networking. It means getting to grips with the major operating systems in use, such as Windows and Linux.

Hackers need to have an above-average grasp of these topics because hacking will often mean finding workarounds in different types of systems.

And you will need to keep up with the latest developments in the field as well. Whenever new software comes out, you will need to understand how it works so that you can pinpoint a weakness in it and fully understand how it operates.

Ideally speaking, you need to have a mind that loves problem-solving and you also need staying power, curiosity and perseverance.

Hacking into systems means having to find loopholes in coding and this can be a painstaking and incredibly boring process at times. It could mean poring over pages of code to find a small weakness that can be exploited.

Hacking Jargon

Hackers have their own lingo and you need to learn some of it if you intend to successfully fit into this world.

Here are some common terms that you will need to know:

- **Exploit:** Refers to a technology or tool that helps you to take advantage of system glitches, bugs and other vulnerabilities. Essentially an exploit is an abbreviated code string that lays the weaknesses in the system bare. They can be used to give you admin privileges, access you are not allowed to have, or to cut off access to authorized users. They are usually the first step that black hat hackers will try. Hackers will usually be able to write their own code in this regard but don't worry too much if you cannot do the same. There are a lot of programs out there that offer generic exploits that you can use instead.

- **Threat**: A threat is something that may be used by a hacker to violate the security of a digital system. Hackers who are involved in shoring up security systems will make a point of looking out for these. These again can be highly personalized by the hacker and are fundamentally intended to breach a system.

- **Vulnerability**: This is what a hacker dreams of. A gap in the code, or glitch in the design that makes it possible for them to get in. This could be in the coded software, in the base design or in the implementation of the program itself. These vulnerabilities allow hackers to access the system as and when they please.

- **Target of Evaluation**: When you hear this term, it is referring to the system that is going to be under attack or that needs to be analyzed. Hackers evaluate the T.O.E. in order to see if there are any weaknesses that may be exploited. They also look for data that makes it easier to break into the system or to crack passwords. Depending on what type of hacker you are, this could be to obtain confidential data such as account numbers, etc. or it could be used to find ways to repair the system and make it less vulnerable to attack. White hat hackers will look for ways to prevent black hat hackers from accessing the system.

- **Attack**: If the system is under attack, it means that it has been compromised as a result of the vulnerabilities within it. The hacker has studied the T.O.E. and found a vulnerability. They may then have written and exploit to take advantage of this error. This is why research is so important. The research phase is where the hacker is going to spend most of their time – they need to identify vulnerabilities that they can take advantage of and this can take a while.

How Do I Get an Exploit to the Targeted System?

There are basically two different approaches when it comes to delivering exploits. These include:

Via Remote Access: In this instance, it is not even necessary to be in direct contact with the targeted system. You can send the exploit to any member within the network and gain access that way. This is a remote hack and the type of hack that we expect most hackers would use.

Via Local Access: This is a little more difficult because it means that you need to have had access to the targeted system at some stage in time. It is, however, the method that most seasoned hackers will employ – it is easier to move around in a system that you already have had access to. This is also why people working at companies have only enough access to the systems to allow them to do their job properly. Should they try to change or delete data that falls outside of their ambit, they would be unable to do so.

This system can be effective at reducing the chances of a local exploit. It should also be stated here that the majority of hacks end up being traced to individuals working within the targeted company. This kind of internal hack means getting as much access to the systems as possible, and even building your privilege level so that you have more access.

Check out the rest of "Hacking - The Complete Beginner's Guide To Computer Hacking: How To Hack Networks and Computer Systems, Information Gathering, Password Cracking, System Entry & Wireless Hacking" on Amazon.

Check Out My Other Books!

Hacking - The Complete Beginner's Guide To Computer Hacking: How To Hack Networks and Computer Systems, Information Gathering, Password Cracking, System Entry & Wireless Hacking

Tor - Accessing The Deep Web & Dark Web With Tor: How To Set Up Tor, Stay Anonymous Online, Avoid NSA Spying & Access The Deep Web & Dark Web

All books available as ebooks or printed on Amazon

www.ingramcontent.com/pod-product-compliance
Lightning Source LLC
Chambersburg PA
CBHW071141050326
40690CB00008B/1532